INSIDE:

A Bit About This Strange Little Project Of Mine ... 3

Ukrainians And Americans Are Done With This War, But It Keeps Escalating Anyway ... 4

This Dystopia Depends On Hiding Inconvenient Truths ... 6

They Lied About Gaza, And They're Lying About Syria ... 8

The Kind Of Ceasefire Where One Side Keeps Firing ... 10

Don't Buy Into Phony Anti-Establishment Schtick ... 12

Stop Supporting Israel If You Can't Watch The Footage Of Dead Kids In Gaza ... 14

Blinken Is Pushing For Ukrainian Teens To Die For US Hegemony ... 16

The Real Villains ... 18

I Have Learned A Few Things ... 20

Assad Is Out, Woke Al-Qaeda Is In ... 22

Another Nation Absorbed Into The Blob Of The Empire ... 24

Taliban In Afghanistan Bad, Al-Qaeda In Syria Good ... 26

„Terrorist Organization" Means Whatever The US Wants It To Mean ... 30

Netanyahu Hilariously Claims Israel Doesn't Seek To Intervene In Syria's Affairs ... 32

The jubilant reaction from the public to the murder of UnitedHealthcare CEO Brian Thompson took the oligarchic class by surprise this month and had one particular billionaire literally sweating in his chair (p42) as his body unintentionally betrayed how painfully aware the ruling elite are of how outnumbered they are.

All works are written by Caitlin Johnstone and Tim Foley. The Caitlin Johnstone project is 100 percent reader-funded.

Visit caitlinjohnst.one for the original articles and their supporting links.

Let Yourself Be Shattered By Gaza ... 34

Some Thoughts On The Mystery Drones ... 36

Meditations On A Six Year-Old Amputee Crawling Through Gaza With The Help Of A Roller Skate ... 38

That Which Can Be Destroyed By The Truth, Should Be ... 40

Peter Thiel Reveals How Scared Oligarchs Are Of The People ... 42

Trump And Israel Can't Wait To Start Bombing Iran ... 44

Drones ... 46

Where Does The Aggression Really Begin? ... 48

Israel Is Killing Civilians In Gaza On Purpose, And It's Not Even Debatable ... 50

A Bit About This Strange Little Project Of Mine

Every so often I like to write out a basic explanation of who I am and what I'm trying to do here. As an entirely reader-funded writer I think it's important to periodically lay out exactly what I'm about so that any patrons or would-be patrons can assess if this weird little project here is something they want to support.

For starters, everything "I" write here under the name of Caitlin Johnstone is actually the work of two people: myself and my American husband Tim Foley. Many of you might know Tim as the male voice who does the readings for all of our articles. While it's my vision and I'm in charge of the editorial direction these works take, Tim co-authors and co-signs everything I publish. Most of the stuff you read here arises from conversations he and I have while nerding out about war, philosophy, humanity, and how to save the world.

Tim and I met in an online discussion group about spiritual enlightenment. He moved out here to Australia to be with me in 2016, and a few months later we found ourselves writing political essays which at the time focused on the Bernie Sanders presidential campaign. After a long series of miracles, mishaps and embarrassments, we somehow wound up doing crowd-funded commentary as a full-time gig.

It was strange and scary suddenly amassing a large following before we'd really had time to learn and grow in our understanding of the world. We'd both spent many years mostly unplugged from politics focused entirely on spirituality and healing, and then all of a sudden we were seized with this powerful impulse to begin writing about the world's problems and had to do so with thousands of people watching us while we were still total neophytes to the political scene. Most people who do things in front of an audience get to spend a long time practicing before they step onstage, but we had to learn on the fly and feel our way into it, and it was frequently both terrifying and humiliating. Eventually we got the hang of it, but we continue to learn and grow.

The basic premise of everything you read here is fairly simple and straightforward: we live in a tyrannical dystopia that's driving humanity to its doom, and we need to wake up from the propaganda indoctrination and egoic delusions which keep us complying with the status quo so that we can use the power of our numbers to overthrow our oppressors and create a healthy world. We come at it from countless angles using all different approaches, but that's the basic message and the idea underpinning it all.

Ideologically we're about as far on the left end of the political spectrum as it gets. Tim was a bit of a US-model libertarian when we first met, but I tricked him into becoming a commie using my feminine wiles. Because we see all of humanity as deeply deluded at this point in history we're reluctant to identify with any particular political faction or group up with any particular clique, but it seems pretty clear that a healthy world where the environment is protected and people's basic needs are met will necessarily entail the complete dismantling of capitalism. We're going to have to transition from competition-based systems to collaboration-based ones where we all work together for the good of every living being.

Our business model is one of the most interesting and unique things about our project. Everything we publish is free to read, and anyone who wants to is encouraged to republish, repurpose and re-use anything we create free of charge. All our income consists of donations from people who support what we're doing and want to help us continue doing it, without expecting anything in return; there are no special perks offered for donating besides our gratitude and your knowledge that you're supporting something you believe in. We try to shape our lives like the kind of world we want to see emerge in the future, and this miniature collaborative unconditional gift economy is one of our efforts at doing that.

For some strange and miraculous reason this peculiar model seems to actually work, and we've been able to dedicate our lives to making ourselves as useful as possible in the best way we know how. It has been a thrilling adventure and a great privilege to do this for a living, and we are so unspeakably grateful to everyone who makes it possible.

Our hope of course is that one day this job becomes unnecessary because the wars, tyranny and abuse have ended and a healthy society has been created. Nothing would make us happier than to become obsolete and unnecessary so that we can hang up the gloves and move on to the next project. That is part of the future we are working toward.

Until then, we'll be here. Writing every day, taking as few days off as possible, and doing everything we can to open eyes and throw sand in the gears of the machine.

Thank you so much for traveling with us, in whatever way you travel.

•

Ukrainians And Americans Are Done With This War, But It Keeps Escalating Anyway
• Notes From The Edge Of The Narrative Matrix •

The IDF dramatically increased its bombing campaign in Lebanon on Tuesday in the hours preceding an expected ceasefire with Hezbollah.

Israel always does this, and it's so gross. Normal people get a ceasefire agreement and think "Good, this means we can finally stop fighting." Israel gets a ceasefire agreement and goes, "This means we have to hurry up and kill as many people as possible before it takes effect."

•

The Biden administration is now pushing Ukraine to lower its minimum draft age from 25 to 18 in order to provide more cannon fodder for the war against Russia.

Polls say that both Ukrainians and Americans want this US proxy war to end, but instead of ending it Washington is pressuring Kyiv to throw teenagers into the threshing machine of an unwinnable conflict.

And we were told this war was all about protecting democracy.

•

Russia keeps getting hit by Ukraine with US-supplied long-range missiles and is now saying that "retaliatory actions are being prepared." This happens as Trump appoints virulent Russia hawk Keith Kellogg as his envoy to the conflict, adding further weight to my concerns that these soaring tensions may continue to escalate after Trump gets into office.

I'll say right now that if all this insane brinkmanship results in Russia hitting Ukraine with a tactical nuke or something I'll be a lot more enraged at the western power structure I live under for giving rise to that horror than I'll be at Vladimir Putin.

•

Don't side with the powerful. Don't side with Israel against the Palestinians. Don't side with the US empire against any nation it targets. Don't side with cops against their victims. Don't side with billionaires and politicians against the people. Don't side with the powerful.

•

Every four years Americans get to choose between the Republican Party and the party that consistently leaves them so disgusted that they then vote for the Republican Party.

•

The way American liberals spent months trying to whip up support and enthusiasm for an administration that was committing an active genocide exposed the disdain western liberals have for non-western lives in ways that will be remembered for generations.

•

Leftist indie media figures tend to drift to the right, either by shilling for liberal establishment politics or by promoting the faux populism of the Trump faction. This happens because when your business model is largely driven by clicks and views, you have an incentive to go where the mainstream numbers are. They don't start off thinking "I can't wait to sell out and covertly promote the interests of the power structures I claim to oppose," they just see their virality go up when they talk one way compared to another and start putting out the kind of content that generates more.

Independent media does not exist in a vacuum, it exists in an information environment that's saturated in empire propaganda which is designed to herd the public into two power-serving mainstream political factions. By changing their output to align with the mainstream liberal faction or the mainstream right wing faction, indie media creators are effectively surfing on the tide of these propaganda streams to carry them into fame and fortune.

This effect is further exacerbated by the fact that people tend to become more right wing the wealthier and more well-connected they become. The idea of fighting a class war against the ruling class is suddenly a lot less appealing when you're a millionaire with a lot of rich celebrity friends and high-level political connections, so you'll naturally find yourself pushing vapid culture war bullshit instead and restricting your criticisms of status quo politics to a much smaller zone. This happens to align perfectly with what the empire propagandists are doing, so you'll still get plenty of clicks and views.

This doesn't happen to you if you actually stand for something and get into indie media for principled reasons, but if you just got into it to have a cool job or whatever then you're just going to do the job thing with it and do what makes you money. It's pretty easy to see who lands where on this dynamic.

Featured image via Adobe Stock.

This Dystopia Depends On Hiding Inconvenient Truths

This civilization is built upon the practice of continuously hiding inconvenient truths out of sight and out of mind. An entire empire held together by compartmentalization and avoidance.

Inconvenient truths are hidden from us in many different ways. They are hidden from our minds using propaganda, indoctrination, censorship, algorithm manipulation, and other forms of narrative control used to manipulate the ways we think about our world.

Inconvenient truths are also hidden from our physical eyes and ears by the manipulation of material reality. We're choking the developing world with plastics as we ship the mountains of garbage the west produces off to poorer countries, for example. If nations had to keep the waste they produce and consume within their own borders, western civilization would either force its corporations to stop offloading their costs of industry onto the environment or find itself buried in garbage. We ship our trash away, out of sight and out of mind, to hide the contradictions and abuses that are built into our capitalist society so we can pretend everything's going fine.

Inconvenient truths are being hidden when laws are passed to force the homeless to relocate away from rich neighborhoods and other places where they are not wanted, or force them all into "tent cities" as Donald Trump is saying he wants to do. There are never any plans to give these people homes or solve the underlying problems which create poverty and homelessness; there are only ever plans to hide the symptoms of the injustices and abuses that are woven into the fabric of the civilization we live in.

Inconvenient truths are being hidden when we condemn the past use of slavery in our own countries while outsourcing immense amounts of wage slavery to the global south, extracting labor and resources from impoverished nations at extortionate and increasingly unfair rates. The suffering, impoverishment, relentless toil and terrible working conditions of these foreign workers are kept out of sight and out of mind while we gorge ourselves on cheap goods and toss our garbage back in their faces.

Inconvenient truths are being hidden by how much more comfortable our rulers are with using violent force in faraway nations compared to here at home. In the western world you might have to worry about being assaulted by a police officer or a SWAT team smashing in your door and killing your dog if you are suspected of selling drugs, but you don't have to worry about your home being bombed or your children being executed by military snipers while playing in the streets. Because foreign nations are out of sight and out of mind, the managers of the western empire think nothing of raining fire down upon them to promote their strategic interests.

We walk around in this perverse dystopia and laugh and joke and act like everything is fine, but everything is not fine. People are suffering and dying at an unimaginable scale because of the systems which allow us to live this way, and if it weren't for the deceitful way this is always being hidden out of sight and out of mind, we would see this first hand right in front of us. And we would be forced to own it.

Western civilization is like a castle on a mountain, and the mountain is made out of human corpses and weeping mothers and starving children, and everyone in the castle pretends that the mountain is not there. It forms the very foundation of everything our society is, but we try not to think about it too hard. It's not just the propagandists who lie to us. We also lie to ourselves.

And it's always been this way. The well-to-do have always hidden themselves away from the suffering of their subjects. Palaces throughout the ages have been islands of paradise amid oceans of human suffering caused by the monarchs who lived in them. Wealthy neighborhoods are always segregated apart from the lives of the poor whose backs they are built upon.

That's the entire western world right now. That's what we are. That's what we're doing. This is a civilization made of deceitful thoughts, deceitful words, and deceitful deeds. Everything about it is fraudulent.

The truth can't stay hidden forever, though. There's only so long we can keep this up. Someday we're not going to be able to keep flailing around looking every direction except at reality, and truth will make itself heard.

Featured image via Wikimedia Commons/CaptainDarwin (CC BY-SA 4.0)

They Lied About Gaza, And They're Lying About Syria
• Notes From The Edge Of The Narrative Matrix •

Al-Qaeda affiliates with a history of receiving western funding have reactivated in Syria along with Turkish-backed fighters to recapture significant amounts of territory in the war-ravaged nation.

It's hard to say exactly what's happening in the moment, but I will say it's mighty convenient how Russia being tied up in Ukraine and Hezbollah being decapitated by Israel leaves Syria once again exposed to the longstanding regime change agendas of the same western empire who's been backing both of those proxy conflicts.

•

Syria is more complicated and harder to understand than Gaza, but if you look into it you'll find mountains of evidence that for many years the US and its allies and partners have been actively fomenting violence, chaos and destruction in that nation to effect regime change. Anyone who denies this is either ignorant or dishonest, as is anyone who calls you a Russian propagandist or an Assad lover for stating this well-evidenced fact.

There are a lot of people who see through the imperial lies about Gaza but still buy into the imperial lies about Syria, largely because the lies about Gaza are so much easier to see through. Immense amounts of propaganda and information ops have gone into framing the violence we've been seeing in Syria since 2011 as a completely organic rebellion against a tyrannical dictator who just wants to murder civilians because he is evil. But if you bring the same sincere curiosity and rigorous investigation to this issue that you brought to the plight of the Palestinians, you will discover the same kinds of lies and distortions which you've seen the western political/media class promote about Gaza being spun about Syria as well — frequently by the same people.

This is how unpacking the lies of the empire tends to unfold for folks. Your eyes flicker open because of some really obvious plot hole in the official narrative like Vietnam, the Iraq invasion, or Gaza, and then once you've seen through those lies you start getting curious about how else you've been deceived. You start pulling on other threads and learning more and more, and then after a while you start seeing the big picture about the US-centralized empire inflicting horrific abuses upon humanity all around the world with the goal of dominating the planet.

If you saw through the lies about Gaza, don't stop there. Keep going. Keep pulling on threads. Keep learning. Stay curious. They lied about Gaza, they lied about Iraq, they lied about Libya, they lied about Ukraine,

and they're lying about Syria too. Don't listen to anyone who tries to dull your curiosity. Ignore anyone who tries to shout you down and shut you up for asking inconvenient questions. Keep waking up from the matrix of empire propaganda until your eyes are truly clear.

●

Boris Johnson told The Telegraph in a recent interview that the west is "waging a proxy war" in Ukraine, which, while obviously true, was once considered by the western political-media class to be a very taboo thing to say.

"We're waging a proxy war, but we're not giving our proxies the ability to do the job," Johnson said. "For years now, we've been allowing them to fight with one hand tied behind their backs and it has been cruel."

For years it was considered Kremlin propaganda to call the war in Ukraine a western proxy war against Russia. Now the line is "Well this is obviously a proxy war so we need to give our proxies more weapons, duh!"

●

We're taught that heroes look like western soldiers and cops taking out bad guys, when really heroes look like Palestinian journalists risking everything to tell the truth about genocidal atrocities that are backed by western governments while western journalists make propaganda.

●

I don't want the Australian government to ban kids from social media, I want the Australian government to stop supporting Israel's genocidal atrocities and stop turning this country into a giant US military base in preparation for Washington's war with China.

●

It should be illegal to force homeless people to relocate. If a rich neighborhood is the best place to sleep rough then the rich should be forced to look at a daily reminder of the dystopia they live in until the underlying problems which cause homelessness have been fixed. You shouldn't be allowed to hide such things to make people comfortable.

All the laws designed to criminalize homelessness and force the unhoused to relocate are just one more way our dystopia hides its abuses and contradictions from public view, the same as propaganda and internet censorship and murdering Palestinian journalists. They want the homeless out of sight and out of mind in the same way their wars and genocides are out of sight and out of mind.

They just want the homeless to go "away", because they can't fix the injustices and inequality which cause homelessness without upending the power structure they rule. They wish all the symptoms of poverty and injustice in our society could be hidden on the other side of vast oceans like their wars are.

Featured image via Adobe Stock.

The Kind Of Ceasefire Where One Side Keeps Firing
• Notes From The Edge Of The Narrative Matrix •

In less than a week of its supposed "ceasefire" agreement Israel has reportedly attacked targets in Lebanon around a hundred times, leading to a single retaliation from Hezbollah on Monday which resulted in zero casualties. As you might expect, Israel is now playing victim and shrieking bloody murder, vowing a major response against Hezbollah for daring to strike back while Israel violated its ceasefire agreement dozens of times.

Apparently this was the kind of ceasefire where only one side has to actually cease firing. This is such a perfect example of everything Israel is.

•

Scrolling through Twitter this morning I saw an Al Jazeera clip documenting evidence that IDF drones have been playing the sounds of crying babies to lure civilians out of their hiding places so they can be shot and killed, and then I saw a photo that an IDF soldier reportedly uploaded to his own social media depicting himself masturbating while gazing at the destruction of Gaza.

I am not a religious person, so I don't really resonate with words like "demonic" and "satanic" to describe Israeli criminality. But at the same time, I kind of get it. What adjectives are there to describe things like this? "Evil" is a pathetic understatement. Language fails.

They're not just depraved, they're creative and enthusiastic about constantly finding new and innovative ways in which to be depraved. I love words and language more than probably anyone I know, but words always fail me on this front.

•

The "rebel" fighters in Syria are now reportedly telling Israeli media that they are grateful to Israel for bombing Syria and fighting Hezbollah, with The Times of Israel quoting an HTS fighter from Idlib as saying "We love Israel and we were never its enemies."

So, I guess take that for whatever it's worth.

•

Imagine going back in time to 2002 and trying to explain to Americans that in a few years the US government is going to start giving weapons to Al-Qaeda in Syria, and then the world will find out about this and just kind of shrug and then completely forget that it happened.

•

It's annoying how many people I see interrupting adult conversations with infantile prattle about whether Assad is a "good guy" or a "bad guy". We're trying to have mature discussions about important world events; stop babbling about Good Guys and Bad Guys like children watching a cartoon show.

•

Antisemitism simply is not a significant threat in our society. It used to be, but it isn't anymore, because our society has changed. There was a time fairly recently when I would've been discriminated against for being divorced from the father of my children. This never happens to me in our present day, because we no longer have the kind of puritanical society where that sort of discrimination occurs. Some fringe religious kooks on the internet might tell me divorce is a sin, but they have no institutional support and normal people think they're ridiculous.

In exactly the same way, the archaic superstitions and prejudices which drove the persecution of Jewish people in previous generations simply do not exist in the way they once did. What you see labeled as "antisemitism" today is 99 percent just people criticizing Israel or fighting back against the oppressive abuses of a genocidal apartheid state, with the remaining one percent being expressions of medieval prejudices against Jewish people from fringe assholes with no political power.

•

The final word on Biden's entire political career is his decision to spend his lame duck weeks backing a genocide and pardoning his son without doing anything at all to pardon real victims of injustice or make things better for normal human beings in any way whatsoever.

Apparently Hunter Biden has been pardoned not just of the crimes he's been accused of, but any unspecified crimes he may have committed over the last eleven years. Which is a bit suspicious, to say the least.

Whatever. I don't even care at this point. This is one of the least evil things this decrepit monster has done over the course of his presidency.

Featured image via Wikimedia/IDF (CC BY-SA 3.0)

Don't Buy Into Phony Anti–Establishment Schtick

I saw a rant from Mehdi Hasan the other day complaining that the way Elon Musk constantly says the media are corrupt and dishonest "has a massive effect not just on trust and polarization in society, but on election outcomes and political messaging."

Hasan said that Musk, Trump and their ilk "have cynically created an unpenetrable [sic] bubble around their followers, primed them against a reality-based universe, [and] pre-emptively undermined any negative stories about themselves."

Hasan is of course correct that the people who listen to Trump and Musk have largely been herded into fact-resistant echo chambers of cult-like loyalty, but it's worth pointing out that Musk's claims about the media are absolutely correct as well. The media are corrupt and untrustworthy, and do indeed promote lies and propaganda all the time. Just because Elon Musk says it doesn't mean it's false.

One great challenge of our time is that while it's becoming common knowledge that western media is propaganda and western politics is a corrupt sham, fake solutions to these problems are being marketed to the mainstream by the same powers responsible for them. Donald Trump himself will tell you that the media are lying and the political establishment is run by swamp monsters, and then say that the solution is to support Republicans and trust right wing media. Elon Musk will go on Joe Rogan and say the same thing. In 2028 AOC will probably run for president campaigning on the Democratic Party version of the same faux-populist message, just as Bernie Sanders did.

This dynamic poses a major obstacle to those who yearn for real revolutionary change. It's becoming increasingly necessary to not just stand against the status quo but against the fraudulent political factions which pretend to oppose it. It's no longer enough to reject establishment politics and media, we also need to reject the fake anti-establishment politics and media which seek to herd a discontented populace away from meaningful revolutionary movements.

There are probably people reading this right now who've fallen into this very trap, who started reading my stuff because they see me opposing wars and criticizing the media and assume I support the same things they support, even as they throw their support behind a fraudulent political movement that's ultimately designed to keep the wars going and make the mass media propaganda more effective. Last time Trump was president I'd always get his fuzzbrained empire simps trying to convince me their guy was ending the wars and fighting against the deep state, twisting themselves into all kinds of cognitive pretzels when I'd present them with hard evidence to the contrary.

It's a challenge to push back against this new iteration of mass deception, but recognizing where it's happening for yourself is fairly simple: just look at what they wind up telling you to support. If at the end of the day they wind up telling you to support Republicans or Democrats, or to support the "good kind" of Republicans or Democrats, or to support any other mainstream western political party, then they're engaged in the exact sort of manipulation I'm describing here. They're trying to corral you away from a real revolutionary political movement and back into the mainstream flock. Into one of the mainstream political parties which are explicitly designed to undermine all the revolutionary changes you seek.

As capitalism continues to decay and inequalities and injustices become more and more pronounced, public discontent with the status quo is naturally going to rise. Because they can't end the political and economic systems the empire is built upon without collapsing it, the empire managers have instead devised ways to funnel that discontentment back into support for status quo politics. They don't just control the opposition, they control the opposition to the controlled opposition.

The empire managers are always a few moves ahead of the masses. There is simply too much power riding on the continuation of the western empire for those in control to allow an authentic revolutionary movement to emerge which could rock the boat. So they give them fake, decoy revolutions to play with while the empire rolls on.

Featured images via Wikimedia Commons.

Stop Supporting Israel If You Can't Watch The Footage Of Dead Kids In Gaza

If you have not spent the past 14 months watching all the footage of dead and mutilated children coming out of Gaza, then you have no business trying to defend Israel and its actions. If you are avoiding looking at the facts, then you have no business talking about them.

Everyone who has spent these past 14 months bringing their attention to the concrete realities of the nightmare in Gaza has been living in an entirely different world than everyone who has not. A darker world. An uglier world. A world where living monsters prowl the earth.

Their dreams are worse. Their insides feel different. They experience the day to day moments of life in a whole other way.

The opinions of such a person about what is happening in Gaza do not have the same value as the opinions of someone who has avoided looking at these things. Someone who has not been watching the videos, looking at the photos, seeing the blown-out, burnt-up bodies, listening to the screaming children, reading the harrowing stories, is not equal in their ability to form lucid assessments about Gaza to someone who has. Their opinions have no merit, and their words on the subject can be dismissed.

Someone who supports Israel's butchery in Gaza but has not spent the last 14 months bearing witness to the daily deluge of footage showing what that support entails is someone whose position is held together by psychological compartmentalization. They are only able to maintain their view of Israel and Palestine because they've been avoiding looking at the raw evidence of exactly what their position means. They're like someone who eats meat but avoids learning about the harsh realities behind how it got to their dinner plate, because they know if they learned the truth about factory farming and saw how livestock are treated in our civilization it would reduce their ability to enjoy their favorite meals. Except with human beings instead of animals.

If you are only able to hold your worldview together by refusing to face the facts about it, then your worldview is garbage and your opinions suck. If you've been avoiding looking at what's happening to people in Gaza while justifying all the death and destruction with some gibberish about human shields and October 7, then everything that comes out of your mouth about this issue is a lie, because it is only made possible by your own untruthful relationship with reality.

If you don't want to face reality, then stop sharing your opinions about it. If you want to hide your head in the sand and dissociate from what's really being done in your name then at least have the decency to shut up and spend your time in your fantasy land like a normal escapism addict. Stop annoying people by babbling about a subject that you cannot even bring yourself to deeply reckon with.

Featured image via Adobe Stock.

Blinken Is Pushing For Ukrainian Teens To Die For US Hegemony
· Notes From The Edge Of The Narrative Matrix ·

US Secretary of State Antony Blinken repeated the US government's new position that Ukraine needs to start sending 18 to 25 year-olds to fight in its war with Russia, telling Reuters on Monday that "getting younger people into the fight, we think, many of us think, is necessary." This comes even as polls have begun showing that Ukrainians favor making a deal with Russia to end this war as quickly as possible.

This is one of those things that looks more evil the longer you stare at it. They're pushing for teenagers to be thrown into the fires of an unwinnable war like it's nothing — like a corporation saying they need to hire more staff to accommodate their growing business. And why? To tie up Russia so that Syria can be turned into a smoking crater and allow the US war machine to focus its crosshairs on Iran and China, with the end goal of total planetary domination. All because some swamp monsters decided after the fall of the Soviet Union that the US must maintain unipolar global hegemony no matter the cost.

Ukraine barely even has anyone in the country from ages 18 to 25 for various reasons (many of which predate this war), but the managers of the US-centralized empire are pushing to scrape out the few they do have and toss them into the landmines and artillery fire just to keep this unwinnable war going for a few more months. Whether they succeed or not, the fact that they even tried is so profoundly psychopathic it's actually hard to wrap your mind around.

You won't see anyone in Tony Blinken's family headed to the frontlines in Ukraine. These freaks see the population of this planet as nothing more than pawns on their grand chessboard, and they will sacrifice them just as casually.

•

Watching the internet light up with joy over the assassination of UnitedHealthcare CEO Brian Thompson has been interesting. We don't know what the motives of the actual shooter were as of this writing, but the disgust and rage the public holds toward wealthy exploitative parasites these days is becoming more and more incendiary.

Watching all this I keep finding myself thinking of that JFK quote "Those who make peaceful revolution impossible make violent revolution inevitable." What are the people meant to do when predatory megacorporations ruin lives by the thousands? Write them sternly worded letters? Vote the corporations out of office? Their options have been closed to them.

•

You can't be anti-racist and pro-Israel; they are mutually contradictory positions. Israel is an apartheid state, arguably the most racist society on this planet. If you support Israel you support racism, whether you admit this about yourself or not.

•

Al-Qaeda in Syria keeps changing its name for the same reason the military contractor formerly known as Blackwater keeps changing its name: it's a rebranding to rescue its damaged reputation, stifle public outcry, and ensure further funding from the US government.

•

The "left" is divided on Syria only in the same way it's divided on Ukraine and other conflicts: Marxists, dedicated peace activists and opponents of the western empire on one side; shitlibs, NATO simps and anarkiddies on the other. The high level of leftish unity we've been seeing between those two groups on Gaza this past year is the exception, not the norm.

You see this split pop up on issue after issue, and it basically boils down to a divide between those who recognize the US-centralized empire as the world's most murderous and tyrannical power structure vs those who swallow western propaganda spin to some extent.

Featured image: State Department Photo by Freddie Everett (Public Domain)

The Real Villains

The CEO of health insurance giant UnitedHealthcare was gunned down by a masked assailant on Wednesday, much to the delight of Americans who've been suffering under their nation's abusive healthcare system and the sociopathic profiteers who make their fortunes exploiting them through it.

UnitedHealthcare has an unusually high rate of claim denials, even compared to its fellow predatory health insurance companies, and as CEO of the company Brian Thompson was personally raking in $10.2 million a year.

The casings on the bullets used to murder Thompson reportedly had the words "deny", "defend" and "depose" written on them, an apparent reference to the "delay, deny, defend" tactics notoriously used by health insurance companies to avoid payouts.

According to Thompson's wife he had been receiving threats from people because of his company's actions, telling NBC News that the threats were from people who were angry about "Basically, I don't know, a lack of coverage?"

That's an actual quote, by the way. The way she phrased it as a question says so much about how psychologically compartmentalized she had been from her husband's predatory behavior. Like the wife of a mob boss who doesn't think too hard about where all the money and gifts are coming from.

The conversations this story has sparked are very interesting. I've seen a lot of posts online highlighting the fact that the murder victim in this case was himself a murderer, and a much more prolific one than any serial killer or mass shooter who's ever lived. The only difference was that his style of murder was protected by the law.

This really nails home the point that the legal system is not intended to protect ordinary citizens from the worst people in our society, it's there to protect the very worst in our society from ordinary citizens. You can see this just by watching the frenetic police manhunt that's underway for Brian Thompson's killer while Thompson himself was walking around a free man, and an obscenely wealthy one at that, despite his having made his wealth via profits reaped from corporate policies designed to deprive sick and injured people of healthcare as frequently as possible.

None of the world's worst people are in prison. Our society is fed a steady diet of movies and shows depicting heroic protagonists fighting villains who abuse and murder people in illegal ways, when in real life the actual villains of our society murder people in ways that are completely legal. None of their abuses are against the law.

Everyone's talking about the murderous practices of US health insurance companies today, and rightly so, but we should also bring awareness to the fact that it isn't just billionaire healthcare corporations who are killing and abusing people at mass scale for profit. Anyone who rakes in billions is building an empire on the blood, sweat and tears of ordinary people. At the very least they are leveraging unfair socioeconomic systems to extract labor from people around the world at extortionate rates, because everyone needs money and most people are born under the unfortunate circumstance of having nothing to sell but their labor. Workers are given the bare minimum slice of the corporate pie in order to maximize profits, in exactly the same way health insurance companies deny claims to maximize profits, keeping huge numbers of people toiling in crushing poverty. And poverty kills. These abuses are exponentially worse in the ways they are inflicted upon the populations of the global south.

That's the bare minimum level of abusiveness you will find in these billionaire corporations — the most profitable ones are far more abusive. They actively work to create more and more war, ecocide, exploitation and inequality, because these things increase their profits. They lobby governments for more wars and militarism around the world because they manufacture weapons of war. They lobby governments to shrink environmental regulations because they maximize their corporate profits by pillaging the earth and externalizing the costs of industry onto the biosphere we all depend on. They lobby governments for fewer worker protections because worker protections eat into profits. They lobby governments for exploitative trade agreements because globalization gives them a steady supply of cheap wage slaves with fewer workers' rights. They lobby governments to privatize services and resources so that they can turn things people are already getting into coercive mechanisms of private profit extraction.

These abuses are the product of the exploitative, profit-driven, competition-based systems under which we live. In a system where it's profitable to sell health insurance and frequently deny insurance claims, you're going to see psychopaths rise to obscene levels of wealth and power by profiteering off health insurance. In a system where war is profitable, you're going to see psychopaths rise to obscene levels of wealth and power by profiteering off war. In a system where ecocide is profitable, you're going to see psychopaths rise to obscene levels of wealth and power by profiteering off ecocide. In a system where exploitation is profitable, you're going to see psychopaths rise to obscene levels of wealth and power by profiteering off exploitation.

Our laws and police forces exist first and foremost to protect these abusive systems. They're not there to protect us, they're there to protect our abusers. They're there to make sure what happened to Brian Thompson happens as rarely as possible, and that people like him are able to abuse people like you and me with total impunity.

•

I Have Learned A Few Things

I have learned a few things in my time on this earth. Not many, but a few.

I have learned that western regime change interventionism is reliably disastrous, and that men like John Bolton and Bill Kristol are always on the wrong side of history when it comes to such matters.

I have learned that organizing human civilization around the pursuit of profit has had devastating consequences for our ecosystem, our health, our hearts, and our happiness.

I have learned that there is an entirely unacceptable amount of human suffering in developing nations, and that it is largely caused by the western power structures we live under and the way our civilization behaves.

I have learned that rich and powerful people pour tremendous amounts of resources into psychologically manipulating the public using all forms of media, and that their efforts to indoctrinate the masses have proven very successful.

I have learned that because our civilization is so saturated in propaganda and our consciousness so indoctrinated, I stand a much better chance of forming an accurate understanding of the world by trusting in my own learning and insight than by trusting in anyone else's.

I have learned that it is possible to awaken from the egoic delusions which are responsible for most of our suffering, and begin moving harmoniously on this planet with an open heart and eyes full of wonder.

I have learned that the self is an illusion and the way most people perceive things like thought, time and separateness is not truth-based, driven instead by wildly inaccurate assumptions about the most fundamental aspects of human experience.

I have learned that it is possible for two people to dedicate their lives to loving each other with total abandon, holding nothing back for themselves and pouring everything they've got into their beloved, without ever becoming depleted because their cup is continuously being re-filled by the other.

I have learned that everything is stunningly beautiful, and that any failure to perceive beauty anywhere is a failure of perception by the beholder.

I have learned that our lives are so much more intimately intertwined than we would ever dare imagine, not just with each other but with every non-human life on this planet.

I have learned that a life dedicated to learning what's true and to expressing truth is the only kind of life that can ever satisfy.

I have learned that I am still learning, and always will be for as long as this body draws breath.

I have learned that the more I learn, the more mysterious life becomes.

I have learned that the more mysterious I allow this life to be, the more enjoyable it is.

The learning continues, even as the conclusions crumble in the radiant light of the mystery, and I stare bewildered at a universe made of question marks.

Featured image via Adobe Stock.

CNN Exclusive

SYRIA'S CIVIL WAR

CNN SPEAKS TO MAIN REBEL LEADER AMID SHOCK OFFENSIVE

CNN NEWSROOM

Assad Is Out, Woke Al-Qaeda Is In

Well it looks like the government of Syrian president Bashar al-Assad is on its way out, likely to be replaced by one or more US puppet regimes depending on whether the nation maintains its current borders or is carved up into separate states. The empire notches another win.

I am not a military analyst, but analysts who are normally supportive and optimistic in favor of Assad like Elijah Magnier and Pepe Escobar are saying this is the end. Assad's whereabouts are unknown as Turkish-backed fighters and al-Qaeda-linked forces with a history of western backing have swept through the country with alarming speed, and now Russia and Iran have joined with the governments of US-aligned nations like Saudi Arabia, Egypt, Jordan and Turkey in calling for an end to the fighting in favor of a political solution. CNN reports that opposition forces have entered Damascus in search of Assad, and footage reportedly shows Assad forces retreating from the area where the president's main residence is located.

The US proxy warfare in Lebanon and Ukraine makes a lot more strategic sense now; by tying up Hezbollah and Russia in other conflicts, the path was opened up for another run on Damascus and a chance to further cut off Hezbollah from supplies. Many pundits on my end of the commentary spectrum had been calling those proxy wars self-defeating and framing them as the desperate flailings of a dying empire which will only accelerate its demise, but now here we are watching the empire score a victory it's been chasing for years, with the western/Israeli stranglehold on the middle east growing tighter than ever.

Meanwhile the press is falling all over itself to support this regime change by promoting the narrative that al-Qaeda is woke now.

CNN just released a coddling softball interview with Abu Mohammed al-Jolani, the former ISIS and al-Qaeda member who leads the Syrian opposition group Hayat Tahrir al-Sham, which is itself a rebranded offshoot of al-Qaeda in Syria. Jolani told CNN that he has reformed from his radical ways of the past, saying, "Sometimes it's essential to adjust to reality," adding, "someone who rigidly clings to certain ideas and principles without flexibility cannot effectively lead societies or navigate complex conflicts like the one happening in Syria."

Now the imperial press are full of headlines like "How Syria's rebel leader went from radical jihadist to a blazer-wearing 'revolutionary'" from CNN, "Syria's rebel leader Golani: From radical jihadist to ostensible pragmatist" from The Times of Israel, and "How Syria's 'diversity-friendly' jihadists plan on building a state" from The Telegraph.

Only a matter of time before we start seeing former ISIS and al-Qaeda members chatting it up on liberal western talk shows with their preferred gender pronouns listed next to their names.

As luck would have it, these "diversity-friendly jihadists" have been telling the Israeli press that they "love Israel" and won't do anything to harm its interests, so it's safe to say that this "revolution" has been about as organically grown as a sheet of crystal meth.

One of the many perks of being the world's dominant superpower is that it gives you the luxury of time. If one regime change operation fails, don't worry, you can just move some chess pieces around and take another shot at it. If a coup attempt fails in Latin America, relax, there will be other coup attempts. If your efforts to grab Syria fail, you can just smash it with sanctions and occupy its oil fields to impoverish it while overextending its military allies in proxy conflicts elsewhere and grab it later.

A good kickboxer throws many combinations with the understanding that most strikes will miss or be blocked or cause minimal damage, trusting that eventually the one knockout blow will get through.

No empire lasts forever, but there's no evidence that this one is going away any time in the immediate future. This ugliness could conceivably drag itself out for generations.

Featured image is a screenshot from CNN on YouTube (Fair Use).

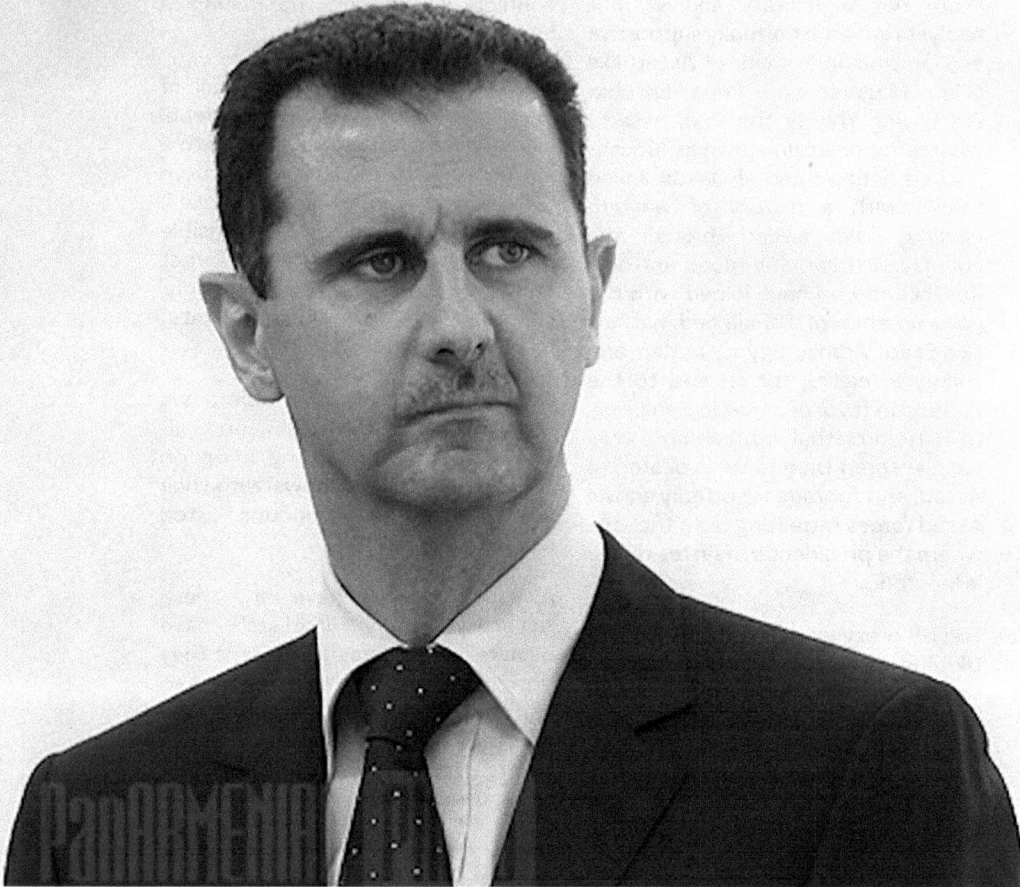

Another Nation Absorbed Into The Blob Of The Empire

Bashar al-Assad has fled Syria to Moscow, where he has reportedly been granted asylum by Russia. The al-Qaeda affiliates who drove him out have declared victory for the "mujahideen" in Damascus. Both Biden and Netanyahu have publicly taken credit for assisting in the regime change, and of course Turkey's Erdogan deserves a heavy share of credit as well.

And yet there's still a bit of a taboo in mainstream western discourse around calling this a regime change operation backed by the US and its allies. We're all meant to pretend this was a 100 percent organic uprising driven solely and exclusively by the people of Syria despite years and years of evidence to the contrary. We are meant to pretend this is the case even after we just watched the US power alliance crush Syria using proxy warfare, starvation sanctions, constant bombing operations, and a military occupation explicitly designed to cut Syria off from oil and wheat in order to prevent its reconstruction after the western-backed civil war.

People get mad at you say this, but it's true. It's just a fact that major world events do not occur independently of the actions of the major world powers who have a vested interest in their outcomes. If my saying this makes you feel uncomfortable, that discomfort is called cognitive dissonance. It's what being wrong feels like.

Maybe it bothers you when people point out the involvement of the US power alliance in Syria, and maybe you would prefer to believe that a plucky band of heroic freedom fighters bravely overthrew an evil supervillain dictator all on their own like some Hollywood movie. But real life doesn't move in accordance with your preferences. In real life, the globe-spanning empire that is centralized around the United States will reliably be deeply involved in such events.

When I say this you may want to believe I am "denying the agency of Syrians," and that "denying agency" is the worst sin a person can possibly commit. But nothing I'm saying actually contradicts the idea that Syrians have their own agency. Obviously there were many Syrians who wanted Assad gone, and obviously there were many people who had their own reasons for fighting him which had nothing to do with the US empire. There is no contradiction between this obvious fact and the well-documented reality that the US-centralized power structure has been balls deep in Syria from the very beginning of the violence in 2011, and that its involvement led to the events we are seeing today.

The claim isn't that the US empire controlled the minds of Syrians and forced them to turn against their government with no agency of their own. The claim is that the empire put a big fat thumb on the scale to ensure that one group of Syrians got their way instead of a different group.

You can argue that western regime change interventionism will lead to positive results this time (so long as you're prepared to ignore mountains of historical evidence consistently demonstrating the opposite), but what you cannot do on any rational basis is deny that western regime change interventionism occurred in Syria.

Western liberalism is funny in that its adherents lean heavily on their ability to psychologically compartmentalize away from the actions of the western empire, and indeed away from the very existence of that empire. The western liberal lives in an imaginary alternate universe where western powers pretty much mind their own business and western leaders passively watch violence and destruction unfold around the world whilst pleading for peace and diplomacy from their podiums. They pretend the empire does not exist, and that it is only by pure coincidence that conflicts, coups and uprisings keep occurring in ways which favor the strategic interests of Washington.

In reality it is impossible to understand what's going on in the world unless you understand that the US is the hub of an undeclared empire which has been working tirelessly to bring the global population under a single power umbrella over which it presides. The few countries who have successfully resisted being absorbed into this imperial blob are the Official Bad Guys we westerners are all trained to hate: China, Russia, Iran, North Korea, and a few socialist states in Latin America. I used to include Syria in this list, but that's over now. Syria has been absorbed into the blob of the empire.

And tomorrow the imperial blob will move its crosshairs on to the next unabsorbed nation. That's the underlying dynamic behind all the major conflicts on earth. This dynamic gets redacted from the mainstream western worldview with the assistance of the western propaganda services known as the mass media, as well as the western indoctrination system known as schooling. This dynamic is redacted from our worldview and hidden from our attention by the plutocrats and empire managers who work to manipulate our information systems, because otherwise we would realize that the US empire is the most tyrannical and abusive power structure on this planet today.

And it unquestionably is. No other power structure has spent the 21st century killing people by the millions in wars of aggression while circling the planet with hundreds of military bases and working continuously to crush any group which opposes its dictates anywhere on earth. Not China. Not Russia. Not Iran. Not Cuba. Not Bashar al-Assad. Only the US empire has been tyrannizing and abusing the world to this extent in modern times.

And now the imperial blob rolls on to absorb its next target, having grown one Syria-sized increment larger after spending years digesting that nation via proxy warfare, sanctions, relentless bombing campaigns from Israel, and a military occupation designed to steal its food and fuel.

Our world cannot know peace as long as we are ruled by an empire that is fueled by endless rivers of human blood. Here's hoping the end of that empire comes sooner rather than later.

Featured image via Pan Photo (CC BY-NC-ND 2.0)

Taliban In Afghanistan Bad, Al-Qaeda In Syria Good
• Notes From The Edge Of The Narrative Matrix •

It's pretty wild how the west went directly from "We need to occupy Afghanistan for two decades to prevent it from being taken over by the Taliban" to "Yay! Syria's been taken over by al-Qaeda!"

•

The IDF has moved to occupy new stretches of Syrian land in the name of protecting its safety and security in the wake of Assad's removal, to approximately zero condemnation from the western power alliance.

One of the dumbest things we are asked to believe about Israel is that the only thing it can ever do to ensure its safety and security when a danger presents itself is to grab more land. Land grabs are always the answer.

So to recap:

Russia invading a country in the name of protecting its security interests from perceived threats on its border = wrong, evil, worst thing ever.

Israel invading a country in the name of protecting its security interests from perceived threats on its border = fine, normal, nothing to worry about.

•

The US is considering removing Hayat Tahrir al-Sham from its list of designated terrorist organizations following the al-Qaeda affiliate's victory in Syria. I have said it before and I'll say it again: "terrorist organization" is a completely arbitrary designation which is used as a tool of western narrative control to justify war and militarism. In effect it just means "disobedient population who need bombs dropped on them".

•

I find it hilarious how empire simps are still shrieking "ASSADIST!" at me for criticizing western regime change interventionism in Syria like that means something. Assad's gone. They can't claim I'm helping him stay in power anymore. This shows they were never mad at me for "supporting Assad" or any of that nonsense; they were always just mad at me for criticizing the western empire, which was all I was ever doing.

Assad's not a thing anymore. Your guys are in power now, and your beloved empire got the regime change it's been chasing for years. You don't get to pretend you're sticking up for the little guy any longer. If you're going to keep simping for the empire you've got to do it right out in the open now; you can no longer mask your bootlicking by hurling bizarre false accusations of treasonous loyalty toward some random middle eastern leader at anyone who criticizes the empire's actions in Syria. You need to find different tactics for your empire apologia.

•

I personally do not believe western interventionism in the middle east leads to positive results and peace, because I am not a newborn baby with a soft squishy head who joined the earth's population yesterday evening.

•

Empire apologists rely heavily on the appeal to emotion fallacy when discussing Syria, because they have no real arguments. They can't counter criticisms of the years of western interventionism which destroyed Syria, so they babble about Assad's victims instead. But no matter how many sad stories you tell and no matter how much sympathy you elicit, it will not amount to a counter-argument against the extensively documented fact that the US and its allies worked to destroy Syria with the goal of toppling Damascus from the very beginning in 2011. You can rend your garments about barrel bombs and prisoners all you want, but it still won't be an argument.

•

I personally don't blame people for misunderstanding what's been happening in Syria all these years. Some of my favorite analysts got Syria wrong in the early years of the war. It's a complicated issue. It's hard to sort out the true from the false, and it's hard to sort through the moral complexities and contradictions of it all as a human being. What matters is that you stay curious and open and sincerely dedicated to learning what's true instead of bedding down and making an identity out of your current understanding.

For years Syria was awash with some of the most complex psychological operations and hybrid warfare the world has ever seen. It's okay if you didn't understand it at first. The world is a confusing place, and is rapidly becoming more so. Just do your best, stay curious, and keep learning.

•

The US House of Representatives overwhelmingly passed the "Crucial Communism Teaching Act", a bill to allow the Victims of Communism Memorial Foundation to develop a teaching curriculum to educate American students on the evils of communism and authoritarianism.

That's right kids, the US government believes capitalism is so self-evidently awesome that it needs to pass laws to indoctrinate children into supporting it. They oppose authoritarianism so much that they'll create entire reeducation programs to train your mind to embrace the freedom of the western empire.

•

It's interesting how Israel uses its extremist settlers to get away with doing things it couldn't get away with doing as a state. The government officially distances itself from these Nazis in front of its western backers, but then lets them do whatever they want and gradually gives them everything they demand piece by piece. This allows Israel to present itself to the west as a liberal free democracy in theory while in practice having a state that's so far to the extreme right it's falling off the edge of the spectrum.

We saw this illustrated recently in the way the IDF collaborated with extremist settlement movement leader Daniela Weiss to help her scout parts of Gaza for future settlement locations, and then released a statement saying that doing so was "illegal and against protocol, and will be handled accordingly." We all know there are unofficial plans to allow those settlements into Gaza at some point, but the official Israeli government position is that it isn't happening.

•

It must be awesome being a supporter of the US empire. You get to see the national leaders you hate get killed and ousted, you rack up win after win, you can trust mainstream western pundits and politicians and believe everything they say, and you get to keep the same worldview they gave you in elementary school.

•

Police have arrested a suspect in the killing of health insurance CEO Brian Thompson. Interestingly the social media of the alleged shooter indicates a political worldview that sits well to the right of the average person who sympathized with Thompson's killer. The further to the right people are, the more likely they've been to sympathize with Thompson.

This disparity in sympathy in the discourse around this shooting has been interesting to watch, because it highlights the contradictions in the US libertarian "non-aggression principle". According to right wing libertarians, the guy who got rich depriving people of lifesaving healthcare committed no aggression. The abuses inherent in a system which prioritizes the generation of profit above all else go unacknowledged in such a worldview. The violence of the tyrants who grow wealthy exploiting the suffering, sickness and struggle of others; who harvest the income of those who can't otherwise afford necessities like healthcare and shelter via insurance fees and rent payments; who plunder the biosphere and externalize the costs of industry onto the ecosystem we all depend on; who leverage the exploitative sociopolitical system known as capitalism to extract labor from workers at extortionate rates; who maximize profits by crushing unions, eroding workers' rights and fighting minimum wage increases — they are seen as entirely legitimate, making any attempt to resist such tyranny entirely illegitimate.

If your worldview doesn't acknowledge that violence isn't limited to the physical act of shooting someone, and that force isn't limited to the physical act of locking someone in a prison cell, then you're not going to see the violence and force in the way the capitalist class leverages inequality, human need, and the law to force the masses to live their lives in ways that make them miserable and unhealthy. You're just going to see a bunch of successful businessmen peacefully going about their business, who are loathed by evil leftists for no legitimate reason. The abusiveness of the means by which those businessmen become wealthy is invisible to you.

•

Things are getting so unpredictable. Nobody saw what happened in Syria coming, or October 7 before that. Used to be the imperial drums would start beating for war with Iraq or wherever, and then later on it would happen. That kind of predictable development you see coming far off in advance is happening less and less now.

Now we're regularly getting blindsided by these rapid explosions of movement. We'll spend months warning about something ugly brewing on the horizon and then something completely unexpected happens somewhere else. I spent years warning a war with Russia was coming but got surprised when it happened when it did in Ukraine because of my own personal biases and blind spots.

I'm learning to observe without making predictions, whether for good things or bad. Nobody knows what tomorrow might bring. Lenin said "There are decades where nothing happens and there are weeks where decades happen," and even that's an understatement nowadays because there aren't decades where nothing happens anymore. There aren't even years where nothing happens. Things are getting way more dynamic and unpredictable. Anything can happen.

The good news is that in a completely unpredictable world, hopelessness is irrational. Anything can happen means ANYTHING can happen. The end of war. The end of the western empire. The end of capitalism. The birth of a healthy and harmonious world. Anything. In a sea of increasing unpredictability, there is no rational basis for ruling out any possibility.

The great unpatterning is upon us. It's a hell of a time to be alive.

•

"Terrorist Organization" Means Whatever The US Wants It To Mean

The US government is simultaneously (A) justifying Israel's land grab in Syria by saying the nation has been taken over by terrorists, and (B) talking about removing those same forces from its list of designated terrorist organizations.

The US podium people have pivoted seamlessly from celebrating the liberation of the Syrian people in the removal of Assad to citing the fact that the nation is now overrun with terrorist factions in defense of Israel's rapid move to militarily occupy large swathes of Syrian land while hammering Syria with hundreds of airstrikes.

At a Monday press conference, State Department spokesman Matthew Miller said these moves by Israel "are temporary to defend its borders" and that Assad's ouster "potentially creates a vacuum that could have been filled by terrorist organizations that would threaten the state of Israel and would threaten civilians inside Israel."

"Every country has the right to take action against terrorist organizations," Miller added.

During a Tuesday press conference Miller further clarified the US position on Israel's land grab, saying, "What precipitated their move into the buffer zone was the withdrawal of the Syrian armed forces, which, as I said yesterday, creates potentially a vacuum that could be filled by any one of the numerous terrorist organizations that continue to operate inside Syria that have sworn to the destruction of the state of Israel."

During the same Tuesday press conference Miller also stated that "there is no legal barrier to us speaking to a designated terrorist group" such as HTS, the group which led the run on Damascus whose leader has been an official in both ISIS and al-Qaeda.

And as it happens the US government has now taken a sudden interest in removing HTS from its listing as a designated terrorist organization, with Politico reporting that there is now "a furious debate playing out in Washington" as to whether or not the group should be removed from the list immediately. Somehow I doubt the debate is actually all that "furious".

So according to one narrative Syria has been liberated by brave freedom fighters and that's wonderful, but according to another concurrent narrative Israel obviously needs to invade Syria because the nation has just been taken over by evil terrorists, and by yet another concurrent narrative those evil terrorists aren't evil terrorists anymore because they're going to be running a US puppet regime.

These are the kinds of contradictions you run into when your policies are guided by the blind pursuit of planetary domination instead of by truth and morality.

In reality, "terrorist organization" is a political designation, not a behavioral one. It has a lot less to do with how an organization acts and operates and a lot more to do with whether or not they advance the strategic interests of the US empire.

Pick any group of non-state actors who fight against the US and its allies and you'll find them on the US government's list of terrorist organizations. Hamas. Hezbollah. They'll even put official state militaries on there like Iran's Islamic Revolutionary Guard Corps. They

used to list the East Turkistan Islamic Movement as a terrorist faction back when the US was expanding its global military presence under the banner of the "war on terror", but they were removed from this listing at the tail end of the Trump administration because the Uyghur Islamist group has been fighting Assad in Syria and may prove useful in the empire's cold war aggressions against China.

Even now the US House of Representatives is moving to ban the US government from using the statistics of Gaza's health ministry to calculate deaths from Israel's genocidal atrocities in the enclave on the basis that the health ministry is run by Hamas, a designated terrorist organization. They need to do this because the Gaza health ministry's death toll is considered so reliable that the US State Department has been using those stats in their own reports.

The group that is committing the genocide necessitating such analysis is of course not a designated terrorist organization.

This is because the label "terrorist organization" is nothing more than a tool of imperial narrative control. In empire language it just means "disobedient population who need bombs dropped on them". If they are determined to no longer be disobedient then they no longer need bombs dropped on them, so they are no longer considered terrorists.

You can kill all the civilians you want using whatever methods you want without being considered a terrorist organization, so long as you are a friend of the US empire.

Featured image is a screenshot from the US State Department YouTube channel.

in Syria's internal affairs;

Netanyahu Hilariously Claims Israel Doesn't Seek To Intervene In Syria's Affairs
• Notes From The Edge Of The Narrative Matrix •

Benjamin Netanyahu is hilariously saying that Israel has "no intention of interfering in Syria's internal affairs."

Only Israel could invade and occupy large stretches of a country, bomb it 480 times in 48 hours, destroy 80 percent of its military defenses, and then claim that it has no intention of interfering in that country's internal affairs.

•

Western regime change cheerleaders are partying about Syria as hard as they can right now because they know soon they're going to have to turn a blind eye to everything that happens in that country for years to come, just like they did with Libya.

•

The new people in charge in Syria have announced that they're going to be opening up the nation's markets and integrating into the global economy, which is one of the least surprising developments in this story so far. This is textbook disaster capitalism which we see in every major imperial power grab on a disobedient nation. Syria is now set to be picked apart and cannibalized by the highest bidder. Looks like meat's back on the menu, boys.

•

TikTok apparently really will be getting banned or sold to more empire-loyal ownership soon. All because the US government doesn't want kids sharing facts about Palestine.

•

People who say violence is never the answer are usually ignoring some massive and hugely consequential forms of systemic violence which gave rise to the violence they're denouncing. It happened with October 7, and it happened with the health insurance CEO.

Yesterday I asked my Twitter followers to complete the following sentence: "Instead of physically attacking the abusive plutocrats who expand their wealth and power by ruining lives and killing people, ordinary citizens should use the other options that are available to them to address such injustices, such as _____."

The responses were interesting. I got a lot of angry replies from people saying I was encouraging violence by posing this question, which is actually pretty revealing if you think about it. I didn't actually encourage violence, I just asked people to list what the alternative options to violence were. If these respondents were aware of options besides violence for dealing with the abuses of wealthy oligarchs, it would never have occurred to them to see my question that way. They themselves see no way to resolve these abuses besides violence; they just think people should submit to continued abuse.

Watching all the widespread support for the CEO's suspected killer Luigi Mangione reminds me of a 2014 essay by venture capitalist Nick Hanauer titled "The Pitchforks Are Coming For Us Plutocrats" warning what he termed his "fellow zillionaires" that "No society can sustain this kind of rising inequality."

"The problem isn't that we have inequality," Hanauer wrote. "The problem is that inequality is at historically high levels and getting worse every day. Our country is rapidly becoming less a capitalist society and more a feudal society. Unless our policies change dramatically, the middle class will disappear, and we will be back to late 18th-century France. Before the revolution."

"If we don't do something to fix the glaring inequities in this economy, the pitchforks are going to come for us," warned Hanauer. "No society can sustain this kind of rising inequality. In fact, there is no example in human history where wealth accumulated like this and the pitchforks didn't eventually come out. You show me a highly unequal society, and I will show you a police state. Or an uprising. There are no counterexamples. None. It's not if, it's when."

Hanauer wasn't speaking out of compassion or altruism but basic self-concern. He wasn't trying to help the poor, he was trying to avoid meeting his maker at the business end of a guillotine blade.

All the rage and bloodlust directed toward these plutocrats does seem to be approaching the boiling point he warned of. I don't know how this is going to play out, but I will say we're at a fascinating point in history.

•

Let Yourself Be Shattered By Gaza

In the suburbs they live with animals
in their homes
who they treat like people and love
like children
while ignoring real children in Gaza.

They'll take a baby dog away from its
mother
and hack its ancient canine
conditioning
to mistake a western nuclear family
for its wolf pack
in order to fill the void in their hearts
which yearns for unconditional love,
all while hoarding their own love
so far deep in their chest caves
that they cannot feel anything for a
Palestinian burn victim
in a bombed-out hospital
who is screaming because there's no
painkiller.

We have so far isolated ourselves
from nature
that we need to fill our homes with
potted plants
and docile, domesticated animals
just to feel whole.

We drink our wine and chuckle at
memes
and talk to our dogs like we talk to
babies
while the world turns to fire
and feral dogs feast on corpses in
Gaza.

These last 14 months have shattered
me.
Shattered me beyond the power of
recollection.

But sometimes it's good to be
shattered.

Sometimes it's good to be dashed to
the floor
and cracked wide open
so that life can get a word in.

Sometimes the heart must be
broken
to smash through the calluses and
cataracts
which accumulate on its surface
and return us to our original
tenderness.

This world will break your heart
and then pour plant medicine into
the cracks.

It will show you a dead Palestinian
child,
and then show you a white kite in
the sky.

It will drop you to your knees
screaming in anguish,
cursing a God you don't even believe
in,
bawling your eyes out,
only to open them and stare in
wonder
at a dandelion growing through the
cracks in the concrete.

It will annihilate everything you
believed about humanity
in a blazing holocaust,
and then leave you blinking and
bewildered
in a mysterious universe of
unfathomable beauty,
the rusted chains of preconception
incinerated from your eyes.

Again and again and again
we are shattered to dust and
scattered to the wind
by the cruelty of this world,
slowly learning that,
if we can fully surrender to the
shattering,
it will return us to that primordial
clarity
we abandoned long ago
when we set out to create this mess
in the first place.

Let yourself be shattered
by heartbreak, by loss, and by Gaza.

Let your whole universe
be reduced to ashes.

Let it all die away,
and then stand up,
and rejoin the fight,
eyes no longer clouded
by anything that could be destroyed
by truth.

*Featured image via Hibr (CC BY-NC-SA
2.0)*

Some Thoughts On The Mystery Drones

Okay I need to jot down some thoughts on the "mystery drone" thing because it's way too interesting a story to ignore.

For those who aren't aware, since mid-November people have been sighting large drones all over the east coast of the United States, and what makes this so interesting is that the US government is claiming they don't know anything about them. Don't know who owns them, where they're taking off from or where they're landing.

They're either lying or telling the truth about this, and either way it's a major story. Either the US government is keeping secrets from the public about huge numbers of drones that have spent weeks flying over populated areas, or they somehow legitimately don't know what's going on with these sightings. Contemplating either of these possibilities should widen your eyes a bit.

And to be clear there really does appear to be something up there. Many of the sightings that are being reported are just the result of a fun news story causing people to look up from their smartphones into the night sky for the first time in years and see things they're not familiar with like planes and stars — but there are also large, hovering aircraft of uncertain origin.

The clearest footage I've seen of these mystery drones so far was presented by NewsNation's Rich McHugh, who actually turned and pointed to one of the craft in the air behind him while reporting out of central New Jersey. It must have been fairly low down because they got a great shot of the thing; it had fixed wings and blinking lights like a plane, but was reportedly only eight to ten feet wide.

McHugh said he and his crew saw some 40 or 50 of the aircraft in the hour they were on location. He interviewed officers from the Ocean County Sheriff's Department, who told him the drones evade detection because they don't give off heat like normal drones, and that one vanished when they tried to pursue it with a police drone. A sheriff named Michael Mastronardy told McHugh that one of his officers reported seeing fifty of these drones flying in off the ocean all at once, after which the US Coast Guard reported seeing a number of the same craft over the water.

Michael Tracey, one of the very few western journalists I have any respect for, went drone hunting and reported seeing "one mystery drone with all red lights, hovering quite low, and another with green and red lights, higher altitude, flying in a straight line."

"It was hovering. If that's a plane, I'm a horse's ass!" Tracey tweeted.

So as far as I can tell this is a real thing and not mass hysteria resulting from large numbers of people suddenly looking up and misinterpreting the lights they're seeing.

But what is it?

As of this writing we're not getting any answers from the US government. The White House, FBI and DHS are all saying that they don't assess that the mystery drones have a foreign nexus or pose a threat to national security, but that they also have no idea what they are. All three departments have released statements saying that "many of the reported sightings are actually manned aircraft, operating lawfully," which sounds intentionally obfuscatory because obviously there are going to be many reports from people misidentifying normal aircraft thrown into the mix, and this is completely irrelevant to all the reported sightings which don't fit that description.

White House spokesman John Kirby was grilled by Fox News' Martha McCallum on the lack of answers on this front, adamantly insisting that he knows absolutely nothing about where these things are coming from or what they're up to.

"I'm telling you we don't know," Kirby said. "We know people are afraid of it. We know people have concerns. We have those same concerns."

New Jersey congressman Jeff Van Drew attempted to sell the idea that what people are witnessing are drones from an Iranian "mothership" which is hanging out off the east coast of the United States, a claim which the Pentagon unambiguously shot down as false. Iran does indeed have ships which carry drones, but obviously the US war machine knows where those ships are located at all times because satellites are a thing.

But aside from Iranian motherships and mass hysteria, it doesn't look like there's much we can cross off the list right now as to what these things could be. I'd imagine if the US government knew they were a foreign threat they'd be doing everything they can to sound the alarm and roll out the war machinery, so maybe we can rule that out too.

Other than that, who knows? The US government is either knowingly lying to the public about its own UAVs or those of a US defense contractor, or it somehow legitimately does not know what these aircraft are, who they belong to, or where they are taking off from and where they are landing. It's hard to imagine how the latter scenario could possibly be the case after all these weeks with all the technology the world's most powerful government has at its disposal for monitoring objects in the sky — but that doesn't necessarily mean it's not true.

For now, I myself am content to not know. It's not often we get to enjoy major news stories about a complete mystery these days, so I'm going to relish this one while the mystery lasts. With all the dark, ugly things that we do know about what's going on in our world, it's nice to have a big strange question mark hovering around in the air for a bit.

Featured image is a screenshot from the NewsNation YouTube channel (Fair Use).

Meditations On A Six Year-Old Amputee Crawling Through Gaza With The Help Of A Roller Skate

It's funny the things that get to you when witnessing the nightmare in Gaza, out of all the horrors you'll see there from day to day. Today I saw a video of a six year-old Palestinian boy whose legs had been amputated dragging himself through his tent camp with the help of a roller skate worn on one of his hands, and it just about destroyed me.

It was one of those inline skates that showed up in the nineties. Rollerblades, we called them. Western boys played with them in summers full of joy and laughter and skinned knees and grass stains. Now a little boy named Mohammad Saeed uses one to help him scoot through the dirt, because his legs were blown off by western military explosives, launched by Israelis who probably played with inline skates when they were small.

This genocide has been going on so long that the child amputees who live all over Gaza are learning strategies to get through life without their limbs.

They did a study recently which found that virtually all children in Gaza now feel their deaths are imminent, and half of those surveyed said they wish to die.

But their lives go on. Even with missing limbs, often amputated without morphine or anesthetic, their lives go on. Crawling their way through muddy tent camps, they go on. They find a way through each day.

It's the kind of thing that might inspire you if it were something you were just passively witnessing instead of something the western power structure you live under is actively inflicting on people. For those of us who live under the shadow of the US-centralized empire it's a bit more emotionally complicated than an inspirational story about the indomitable spirit of the Palestinian people, because it's also a story about how we failed to stop this from happening.

When we look at Mohammad Saeed crawling through the dirt on his leg stumps with the help of a roller skate, we are seeing our own civilization reflected back at us. A genocidal dystopia of complete moral bankruptcy. This is what we have become. This is what we have allowed our rulers to turn us into.

Oh Mohammad, I am so sorry. I am so sorry that we allowed it to come to this. I am sorry that your legs were taken from you, and I am sorry for everything else that has been taken from you on top of them. Your parents maybe. Your siblings maybe. Certainly some loved ones. Obviously your home, and obviously your childhood.

I have nothing to offer at this time, either to my readers or to Mohammad Saeed, apart from my own sorrow. Some days all you can do is pour your heart out on the floor and warn passersby to try not to slip on it, tears streaming down over the gaping hole in your chest.

None of this is right, and I don't feel like pretending it's right. I don't feel like trying to put a positive spin on it or say it's all going to get better. Some things are just terrible, and it's okay to feel terrible about them. Feelings are meant to be felt. It's sad and it's enraging and it's shameful and it's damning, and absolutely nothing else.

We live in a world of such breathtaking beauty and such jaw-dropping savagery. Explosions of love hiding behind every molecule in a society that is ruled by true monsters.

We are big enough to hold these paradoxes. We are big enough to feel the majesty of creation and the gut-punch of genocide. The wet, juicy, sloppy love for our fellow human beings and the horror at how cruel we can be to one another. The exhilaration of life on this strange blue planet and the crushing grief of failure after failure to make things a little better here.

Both the good and the bad are allowed to flourish in this world. Clearly. I have no answers or miracle cures for this. We do our best to be decent people and get through each day. We pick up our skate and crawl on.

Featured image via @translating_falasteen and @karim_alhassani1

That Which Can Be Destroyed By The Truth, Should Be

"That which can be destroyed by the truth, should be."

This is a line by fantasy author PC Hodgell, though it's often misattributed to Carl Sagan.

I think about this quote a lot.

I think about it when reflecting on the way Israel is exterminating Palestinian journalists in Gaza while keeping western journalists out of the enclave to prevent the world from learning the truth about what the IDF is doing there.

I think about it when reflecting on the mountains of government secrecy with which the western empire protects its information interests, imprisoning whistleblowers and persecuting journalists who try to expose the truth about its criminal actions around the world.

I think about it when reflecting on the nonstop deluge of empire propaganda that public consciousness is hammered with to manipulate the masses into accepting the global leadership the US-centralized power structure.

I think about it when reflecting on the US war machine and how all the military operations of Washington and its allies are always justified by lies.

I think about it when reflecting on dysfunctional relationships that are held in place by secrets and dishonesty, preventing the ones being deceived from freeing themselves and finding their way into a life of authenticity.

I think about it when reflecting on the ego and how easily its illusory nature can be seen with a penetrating insight into the truth of how human perception and cognition are really operating.

There are times when withholding the truth would be in the highest interest. Someone lying to the police to protect someone from unjust persecution at the hands of an unjust system. A journalist protecting a source by obfuscating the truth from government agents. A battered wife lying to her husband to calm him down. An abused child lying to their abuser about what they've been doing.

But as near as I can tell the only times when withholding the truth is in the highest interest is when there's an abusive power dynamic at play and the person in the down-power position is using untruth to protect someone in an unjust situation which should not exist in the first place. In all other instances, truth is best.

Truth is the great equalizer. It makes the abuses of the powerful much more difficult to execute, and gives the disempowered much more power. This is why our rulers are constantly working to expand surveillance and eliminate the privacy of ordinary citizens while increasing government secrecy to allow themselves to hide the truth, when in a healthy society it would be the exact opposite. In a healthy society ordinary members of the public would have enshrined privacy protections against the government, and any governmental systems would be as transparent as air.

In a healthy society there would be a direct one-to-one correlation between power and transparency. The more power you have the more transparency should be required of you, and the less power you have the more secrecy you should be shielded with. This would protect ordinary citizens from abuse at the hands of the powerful, and prevent the powerful from becoming abusive toward the citizenry. We know this is true because all the most abusive power structures work constantly to reverse this dynamic to the furthest extent possible.

A healthy society will be a truth-based society. It's hard to imagine what a society that is guided by truth would look like, because we live in a society that is made of lies. If deceit magically became impossible today, all our institutions would crumble by tomorrow. A truth-based society would mean the total destruction of all that is familiar to us right now. But that which can be destroyed by the truth should be.

Truth can be scary, because in any situation sustained by falsehood, truth is a destructive force. It can cause political upheaval. It can end relationships. It can annihilate egoic delusion. Any of these will typically feel like a giant leap into the unknown, and are generally terrifying for exactly that reason. But this is the only path toward health.

If we are to survive on this planet, eventually we're going to have to take that leap. Eventually we're going to have to become a truth-driven species. Everything about our current status quo will resist this movement — the untruth in our current power structures, and the untruth within ourselves.

Maybe we won't take that leap until things get so bad that the unknown looks less terrifying than what the familiar has become. Maybe we will find our courage before it comes to that point. But we're going to have to jump for it eventually, or we will go the way of the dinosaur.

And if it does come to that, if we are collectively unable to take the leap because we value our lies more than our lives, that too will reveal a truth to us about who we are and what we were always made of. One way or the other, truth will have the final say.

That which can be destroyed by the truth should be. And, eventually, will be.

Featured image via Adobe Stock.

Peter Thiel Reveals How Scared Oligarchs Are Of The People

Billionaire Peter Thiel had a fascinating televised moment the other day when asked by Piers Morgan what he thought about the public making a hero of the man suspected of murdering health insurance CEO Brian Thompson. The way he stumbled and stuttered when trying to answer the question gives a lot of insight into how terrified such people are of the public turning against them one day.

"And to those who think this shooter is a hero, because he did it because he said this healthcare executive is presiding over a healthcare system which kills thousands of Americans by denying them cover, what would you say to them?" Morgan asked.

Thiel paused for a long time, and then stuttered for a long time, and then eventually got out the words, "It's, I don't know what, what to say? I, I think I still think you have, you should try to make an argument. And I, I think this is, this is you should, you know, there may be things wrong with our health care system, but you have, you have to make an argument, and you have to try to find a way to convince people and and change, change it by by that, and this is, you know, this is not going to work."

For those who don't know, Thiel is a proper deep state oligarch who owes his vast fortune to his enmeshment within the US military-intelligence machine. His company Palantir is a CIA-backed surveillance and data mining tech company with intimate ties to both the US intelligence cartel and to Israel, playing a crucial role in both the US empire's sprawling surveillance network and Israeli atrocities against Palestinians. He backed Trump in 2016, and Vice President-Elect JD Vance was a protégé of his, so this man is thoroughly entrenched in the halls of power.

Thiel's blustering response when asked what he thought about the public support we are seeing for the practice of assassinating health insurance CEOs reveals a lot about the kinds of things that keep men like Peter Thiel up at night.

Plutocrats like Thiel are constantly thinking about the fact that ordinary people vastly outnumber them and can kill them at any time. They think about it way more often than ordinary people do. It's a point that they are acutely aware of at all times. It consumes their attention. They are always working on manipulating public consciousness to ensure that we don't think as much as they do about how many more of us there are of them, and how we don't have to put up with their domination of our society if we don't want to.

As Michael Parenti once put it:

"I tell students when they say, 'Oh they don't care what we think. They ignore us', and all that, and I say, 'Oh no, no. That's the only thing they care about you. The only thing they care about you is what you're thinking. They don't care if you eat correctly, they don't care how your living conditions are, they don't care that they've built up an inhuman and irrational traffic system that's strangulating us and polluting our air, they don't care about anything. The only thing about you they care about is what you're thinking. In the morning, they start, 'What's going to be the story today? How do we manipulate, how do we control, how do we contain, how do we influence, how do we act upon what it is that they have in their minds?'"

Manipulating public consciousness is of existential importance to the ruling class, because no matter how many billions of dollars you amass, at the end of the day you're still a soft skin sack of blood and bones like anybody else, and you share a society with huge numbers of people who can very easily hurt you if they want to. That's why our minds are constantly being hammered with propaganda into accepting the status quo politics upon which our rulers have built their kingdoms.

But we're seeing the propaganda losing its grip on our minds. Hollywood tried to train people to believe heroes look like soldiers and cops, or billionaires using their wealth to become Iron Man and Batman, and then the people chose as their hero a guy who was arrested for shooting a health insurance CEO. The other day a DJ threw up pictures of the suspected shooter Luigi Mangione during his concert and drew cheers from the crowd — and this was at a Disney-themed show.

So that's why the empire managers are pushing to get their killer robots up and running as quickly as possible.

Israel is reportedly preparing to deploy dozens of weapons systems in the West Bank which are capable of firing deadly rounds without human intervention, meaning fully autonomous killing machines as opposed to remote-controlled. These killer robots have already been in use on Israel's border with Gaza.

Various military robots have been tested in Gaza since Israel's onslaught on the enclave began last year, and now they're expanding the field testing of their murderbots to the West Bank as well. Of all the horrible things Israel and its western backers do to the Palestinians, among the most evil is the way they use them as lab rats to field test new weapons systems so the rest of the empire can learn how effective those systems are.

You may be sure that empire managers like Peter Thiel are watching these developments with keen interest. Militarized robots are the anti-guillotine. They're the final solution to the ancient "there are a lot more of us than there are of our rulers" problem. Everyone with wealth and power has been eyeing their incremental rollout with intense interest while trying to play it cool.

So at this point we're essentially looking at a race to see if the oligarchic empire can manufacture the necessary environment to allow the use of robotic security forces to lock their power in place forever before the masses get fed up with the increasing inequalities and abuses of the status quo and decide to force a better system into existence.

It will be interesting to see how this plays out.

Featured image is a screen shot from Piers Morgan Uncensored (Fair Use).

Trump And Israel Can't Wait To Start Bombing Iran
• Notes From The Edge Of The Narrative Matrix •

Both Israel and the incoming Trump administration are reportedly eager to start bombing Iran ASAP now that Assad's out of the way.

Israeli media reports that the IDF now sees airstrikes on Iran as much easier to execute now that its pilots don't have to worry about Syrian air defenses along the way, while The Wall Street Journal reports that the Trump team is weighing its options for airstrikes on Iran to prevent it from obtaining a nuclear weapon (which there's no evidence Iran is currently trying to do).

A new article from The Washington Post titled "Syria's collapse and Israeli attacks leave Iran exposed" reports that "Israeli Prime Minister Benjamin Netanyahu has signaled a desire to capitalize on gains against Hamas and Hezbollah and take on Tehran more aggressively under a new U.S. administration." The article notes that Trump has expressed openness to war with Iran, saying that "anything can happen".

This comes as the al-Qaeda affiliates who captured Damascus assure the world that Syria will no longer allow itself to be used as a launchpad for attacks against Israel.

After Assad was ousted I got a bunch of weirdos in my comments claiming that Israel was somehow sad about this development, because Israel and Assad were secretly on the same side. This is one of the dumbest conspiracy theories I've been asked to believe in a long time, and I was asked to believe it not by crazy QAnoners or the liberal mass media but by a sector of pro-Palestine leftoids who also love NATO.

•

The US hates al-Qaeda, then loves al-Qaeda, then hates al-Qaeda, then loves al-Qaeda. They split up, they get back together, they split up again. "We were on a break!" "We were not on a break!" Will they or won't they? Keep watching and find out!

•

Fake revolutions everywhere you look. Hooray, the brave freedom fighters ousted the dictator in Syria! Hooray, Donald Trump is fighting the Deep State! Hooray, Bernie Sanders and AOC are transforming the Democratic Party and fighting for economic justice!

As the need for real revolution becomes more and more urgent, we're seeing more and more fake revolutions designed to keep the status quo in place. People's rage against the machine is harnessed by phony billionaire populism and shitlib progressivism so that their political energy can be fed right back into the machine. People are trained to cheer for foreign rebels who are backed by the CIA and fight to expand the might of the US empire instead of for the groups around the world who are fighting against imperial domination.

They funnel our attention and energy into fake revolutions to keep us from fighting a real one. The more discontented the public becomes, the more existentially necessary it will be for them to do this. The longer we keep getting redirected into political dead-ends by those who benefit from the imperial status quo, the longer the imperial status quo will keep abusing us all.

•

Israel supporters will tell you antisemitism is one of the biggest problems in the world and then if you ask them for examples of where dangerous antisemitism is occurring in our society they'll list things like the United Nations, Amnesty International, Ireland, and the pope.

•

I often see questions like "Why are the billionaires destroying the world like this? What's the point of amassing all that wealth if you're just going to spend the rest of your life in some underground bunker?"

Such questions assume a level of rationality I don't believe these people possess. Billionaires are driven by unconscious, irrational forces within themselves, not by rational concerns. Becoming a billionaire is itself an irrational thing to do; nobody needs that much money. Nobody's safety, security, or quality of life is significantly improved by having billions of dollars instead of millions. No matter how much wealth you control, you can only drive one car at a time, wear one suit at a time, live in one house at a time. Past a certain level, accumulating more money becomes an absurdity by any possible metric.

People who amass that much wealth aren't behaving rationally — they're trying to fill a gaping hole within themselves that can never be filled. They're reacting to early childhood trauma and compelled by dysfunctional psychological coping mechanisms. They're subconsciously trying to compensate for believed stories of deficiency and lack; trying to chase after their long-dead father's approval; trying to feel a sense of control in a world which felt very threatening to them when they were small. They're not even acting based on any real concern for their own future, so why would they act based on concern for the future of the planet?

The obscenely wealthy people who rule our world are destroying it not out of stupidity or spite, but out of unconscious compulsion. A heroin addict doesn't keep using because they don't understand that heroin is bad for them or because they hope to overdose one day, they keep using because their addiction is driven by inner pain and psychological forces within themselves which they have not yet brought into consciousness. Becoming a billionaire and becoming a heroin addict are both irrational destructive behaviors driven by irrational internal dynamics. The only difference is that the billionaires are taking the rest of us with them.

Featured images via Wikimedia Commons.

Drones

Drones fill the air and block out the natural sky.

Drones armed with sniper rifles fly over Gaza at night playing the sounds of crying babies to lure civilians out of hiding.

Drones surveil protest movements and give nightmares to grandmothers in New Jersey. Drones with facial recognition technology keep a lifeless eye on us to make sure we are all in our proper places at all times.

Drones for kids as Christmas presents. Free drone in this box of Lucky Charms. Your daughter is so intelligent, maybe someday she will girlboss her way into a job at Lockheed Martin designing military drones to help kill impoverished foreigners.

Drones hover over crooked towers flashing bright signs for Products, Products, Products. Drones hover over suburban houses ruled by fathers with horrible hands. Drones hover over armies of mechanical dogs pouring out into the streets in the moonlight.

A murder of drones in the dead tree at sunset. Flocks of drones migrating to the global south for winter. The sky used to be ruled by living beings. Now it is ruled by drones.

Our birds are being replaced by machines. Our stars are being replaced by Elon Musk satellites. Our minds are being replaced by algorithms. Our hearts are being replaced by social media trends. Our world is being replaced by screens. Our creative genius is being replaced by AI slop.

That sacred green thing within us is being paved over with microchips. Our roots into our mother planet are dying. At night we pray to false old gods and false new gods while we strangle our creator with plastic, and then we count the passing drones to fall asleep.

Featured image via Pexels.

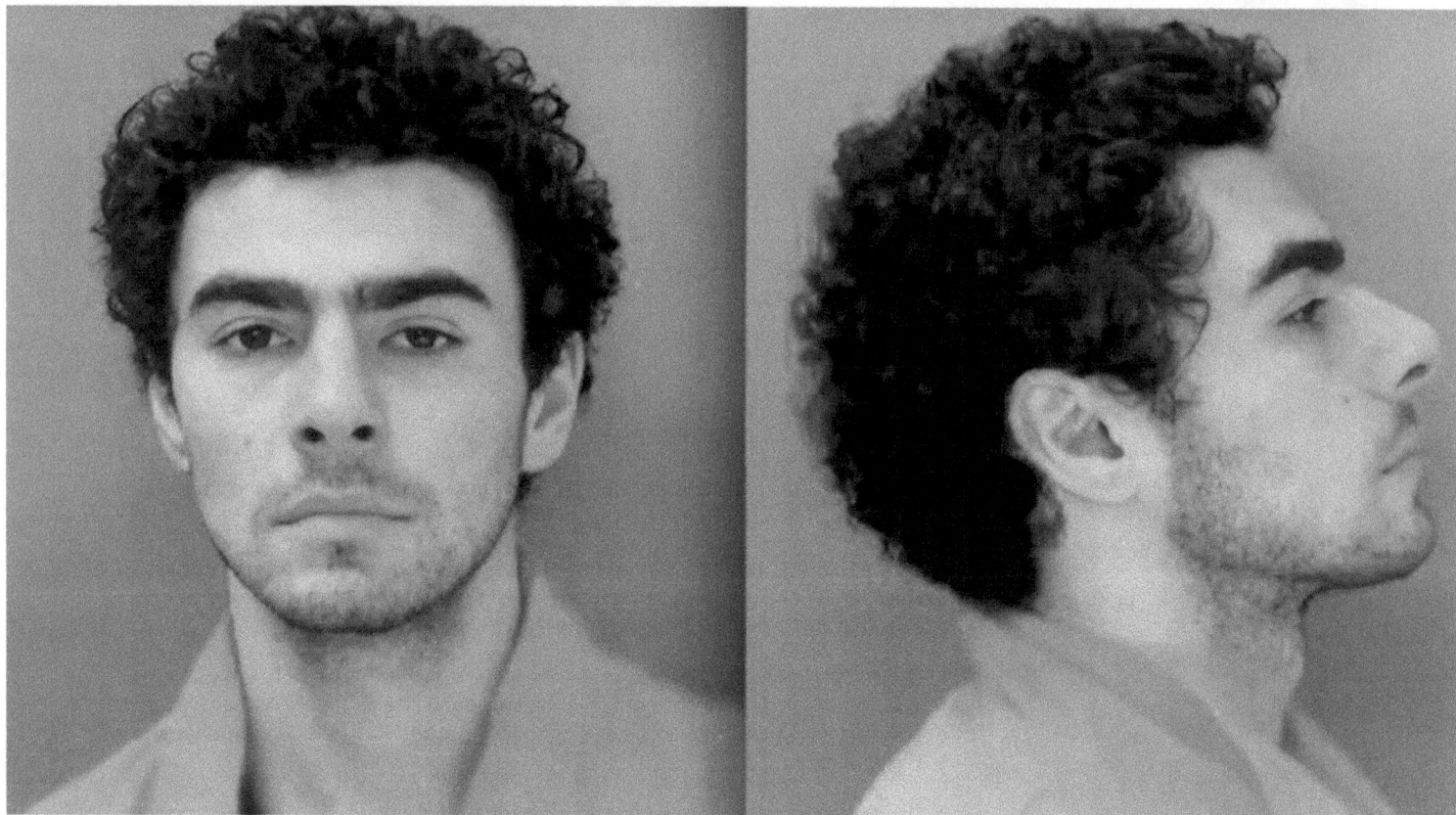

Where Does The Aggression Really Begin?

New York prosecutors have charged Luigi Mangione with "murder as an act of terrorism" in his alleged shooting of health insurance CEO Brian Thompson earlier this month.

This news comes out at the same time as a Haaretz report titled "'No Civilians. Everyone's a Terrorist': IDF Soldiers Expose Arbitrary Killings and Rampant Lawlessness in Gaza's Netzarim Corridor." The report contains testimony from Israeli troops that civilians are being murdered in Gaza and are then being retroactively designated as terrorists to justify their execution.

"We're killing civilians there who are then counted as terrorists," a recently discharged officer told Haaretz.

These two stories together say so much about the way the label "terrorist" is used under the US-centralized power umbrella.

The guy who shot the health insurance CEO is a terrorist, but the people systematically slaughtering civilians in Gaza are **not** terrorists. The people fighting against those who are slaughtering the civilians **are** terrorists, and noncombatants are being categorized as belonging to this terrorist organization in order to justify killing them. The al-Qaeda affiliates in Syria **were** terrorists, but now they're a US puppet regime so soon they **won't** be terrorists — but they need to be designated terrorists for a little while longer because the claim that Syria is crawling with terrorists is Israel's justification for its recent land grabs there. The Uyghur militant group ETIM used to be a terrorist group, but now they're **not** a terrorist group because they can be used to help carve up Syria and maybe fight China later on. The IRGC is a military wing of a sovereign nation, but it counts as a terrorist group because of vibes or something.

Is that clear enough?

Really the label "terrorist" is nothing more than a tool of imperial narrative control which gets moved around based on whether or not someone's use of violence is deemed legitimate by the managers of the empire. Because Mangione's alleged crime has ignited a public interest in class warfare, the label "terrorism" is being used to frame it as an especially heinous act of evil against an innocent member of the public.

The empire's favorite trick is to begin the historical record at the moment its enemies retaliate against its abuses. Oh no, a health insurance CEO was victimized by an evil act of terrorism. Oh no, Israel was just innocently minding its own business when it was viciously attacked by Hamas. Oh no, Iran attacked Israel completely out of the blue and now Israel must retaliate. Oh no, Russia just launched an entirely unprovoked war on Ukraine.

Everything that led up to the unauthorized act of violence is erased from the record, because all of the violence, provocation and abuse which gave rise to the unauthorized act of violence were authorized by the empire. Authorized aggression doesn't count as aggression.

Whoever controls the narrative controls the world. If you control the narrative you can control not only when the historical record of violence begins but what kinds of violence qualify as violence. Killing people by depriving them of healthcare because denying healthcare services is how your company increases its profit margins? That's not violence. Inflicting tyranny and abuse upon a deliberately marginalized ethnic group in an apartheid state? That's

not violence. Violence is when you respond to those forceful aggressions with forceful aggressions of your own.

If we are to become a healthy society, we're going to have to stop allowing some forms of violence, aggression and abuse to be redacted from the official records while others are listed and condemned. Those who care about truth and justice account for **all** forms of violence, aggression and abuse, not only those which inconvenience the rich and powerful.

It is an act of aggression to do things which sicken and impoverish others in order to advance your own wealth.

It is an act of aggression to pollute the biosphere we all depend on for survival in order to increase your profit margins.

It is an act of aggression to use your wealth to manipulate your nation's politics in ways which exacerbate inequality and injustice.

It is an act of aggression to maintain an apartheid state which cannot exist without nonstop violence.

It is an act of aggression to surround the earth with military bases and encircle nations which disobey your dictates.

It is an act of aggression to try to rule the world using military violence, proxy conflicts, staged coups, threats, starvation sanctions, and financial and economic coercion.

These are all acts of aggression, and any retaliation against them will never be an unprovoked attack. As we move into the future while these abuses exacerbate, it's going to become very important to maintain an acute awareness of this.

Featured image via Pennsylvania Department of Corrections

Israel Is Killing Civilians In Gaza On Purpose, And It's Not Even Debatable
• Notes From The Edge Of The Narrative Matrix •

Just so we're all clear, it is a fully established fact that the IDF is directly, deliberately killing civilians in Gaza. There was a time in the early days of the genocide when this could be disputed, but that is no longer true. The facts are in and the case is closed. It's happening.

Israeli soldiers are telling the press that they've been knowingly killing civilians and then falsely categorizing them as terrorists afterward. Countless doctors have testified to routinely encountering dead and wounded children who've been shot in the head by Israeli snipers. Israeli media reports have revealed that the IDF is intentionally targeting civilian infrastructure and using AI systems to specifically target suspected Hamas members when they are at home with their families instead of out on the battlefield.

The debate is over. The "human shields" argument has been completely, thoroughly debunked. If you still deny that this is happening, its because your worldview is so false that it requires you to deny facts and reality.

•

We were fed lies about what happened on October 7. We were fed lies about the Israeli abuses which led to October 7. We've been fed lies about what's been done for the last 15 months under the justification of October 7. And yet Israel's defenders still expect to be taken seriously when they babble about October 7 in response to criticisms of Israel's actions.

•

It doesn't have to be this way. We're fed mountains of stories by the rich and powerful explaining why things must remain as they are — but they are only stories.

Every sociopolitical status quo throughout history has had power-serving narratives explaining why things are as they are and justifying why the people in charge live so much more comfortably than the ordinary folks doing the real work in this world. People used to be told that kings received their authority directly from God, and were therefore better and more worthy than the unwashed masses. Today we have different rulers with different narratives justifying their rule and explaining why vast inequality is fine and good, but those narratives are exactly as fictional as the old stories about the divine right of kings.

Today we are trained to believe that the plutocrats who rule our society attained their vast fortunes through hard work and clever innovation, and are entitled to every penny because they are the most productive members of our society. Just as the peasants of old were taught about the divine right of kings, we are taught that capitalism is the most fair and equitable of all possible systems and that the US-led world order ensures that freedom and democracy will be protected and promoted for the benefit of all.

These are all made-up stories, no truer than the story that monarchs were imbued with magical king powers by an invisible deity because their blood was special. But they are treated as serious facts by those who are responsible for training us how to think, and by those who swallow this indoctrination.

In reality we can change how things are whenever we want, and there's no good reason not to. There are a whole lot more of us than there are of our rulers, and the oligarchs and empire managers who currently hold the steering wheel are destroying our biosphere while increasing inequality and exploitation and pushing us toward nuclear war on multiple fronts.

We have the ability to wrest that steering wheel away from them any time enough of us work up the will to do so. All the stories to the contrary we might believe are just fictional thought-fluff that our rulers put in our minds for their own benefit.

•

There's nothing wrong with being politically homeless at this point in history. Humanity as a whole is still wildly confused and dysfunctional in this particular slice of spacetime, and even the very best political factions are dominated by highly neurotic people who take no responsibility for their psychological state and internal clarity. If you've found a political party or faction you trust then that's great, but if you haven't then it is perfectly fine to stand as an individual while throwing your support behind worthy causes and movements on a case-by-case basis as they emerge without permanently hitching yourself to anyone else's wagon.

We've still got a long way to go in maturing as a species, and it might be a while before a unified political faction arises that you can trust to consistently move in the highest interest.

Featured image via Wikimedia Commons/IDF.

https://www.caitlinjohnst.one